Tons of Trucks!

ICE CREAM TRUCKS

By Luke Harasymiw

Gareth Stevens PUBLISHING

Please visit our website, www.garethstevens.com. For a free color catalog of all our high-quality books, call toll free 1-800-542-2595 or fax 1-877-542-2596.

Library of Congress Cataloging-in-Publication Data

Names: Harasymiw, Luke, author.
Title: Ice cream trucks / Luke Harasymiw.
Description: New York : Gareth Stevens Publishing, [2020] | Series: Tons of trucks! | Includes index.
Identifiers: LCCN 2019009899| ISBN 9781538245132 (pbk.) | ISBN 9781538245156 (library bound) | ISBN 9781538245149 (6 pack)
Subjects: LCSH: Ice cream trucks–Juvenile literature.
Classification: LCC TL230.15 .H3669 2020 | DDC 381/.41740284–dc23
LC record available at https://lccn.loc.gov/2019009899

First Edition

Published in 2020 by
Gareth Stevens Publishing
111 East 14th Street, Suite 349
New York, NY 10003

Editor: Therese Shea
Designer: Katelyn E. Reynolds

Photo credits: Cover, pp. 1, 13, 23 Leonard Zhukovsky/Shutterstock.com; p. 5 mini_citizens/Shutterstock.com; p. 7 anaglic/Shutterstock.com; pp. 9, 24 (wheel) StefaniaArca/Shutterstock.com; pp. 11, 24 (freezer) © iStockphoto.com/Supersmario; pp. 15, 17, 19 Hero Images/Getty Images; p. 21 Africa Studio/Shutterstock.com.

Printed in China

CPSIA compliance information: Batch #CW20GS: For further information contact Gareth Stevens, New York, New York at 1-800-542-2595.

Contents

This is my toy truck.
It's an ice cream truck!

Octan
Ice Cream
Flavors

This is a real
ice cream truck!

CHILDREN
SLOW
CROSSING
"THE REAL DEAL"
SMOOTHIE INC.
FUN-TIME
FUN-TIME
SUNDAES · SHAKES
RETA
FLAG

Ice cream trucks carry treats. They are stores on wheels!

homemade european ice cream
SLUSHIE
fresh

An ice cream truck
has freezers.
Freezers keep
ice cream cold.

Many ice cream trucks
play music.
We hear it on the outside.

"the
Best"
SHAKES · SUNDAES
ICE COLD WATER
75

We can hear music!
The ice cream truck
is coming!

DAIRY
HUT
POPSICLE
CONES

We wave to the driver.
He stops the truck.

"THE BEST IN SOFT ICE CREAM"
DAIRY HUT
SUNDAES

There are so many treats!
We buy ice cream.

DAIRY HUT

I share with my dog!

I love ice cream!
I love this truck!

Soft Ice Cream

Words to Know

freezer

wheel

Index